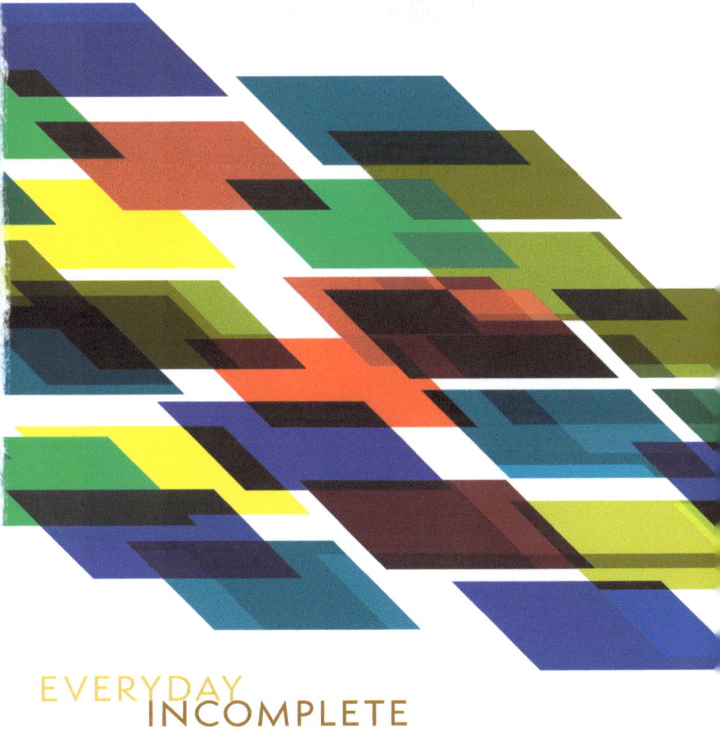

EVERYDAY
INCOMPLETE
LETTERS
for CHRISTIANS

LETTERS *for* CHRISTIANS

Tiekie PRESS

Letters for Christians series
Everyday Incomplete Letters for Christians

Copyright © Pieter de Kock, 2025
All rights reserved.

First published 2025 by Tiekie Press

ISBN 978-1-0686586-4-8

Edited and typeset by Copy–editing Services
https://copy-editing.org/

Cover design by Pieter de Kock

EVERYDAY INCOMPLETE

for

Marthinus

I will say of the Lord,
"He is my refuge and my fortress,
my God, in whom I trust."
—Psalm 91:2 (NIV)

LETTERS *for* CHRISTIANS

FOREWORD

The quote, "I would have written a shorter letter, but did not have the time" is sometimes attributed to Mark Twain, but seems to be more reliably credited to Blaise Pascal in his Lettres provinciales of 1656-7. It reminds us that it is much more difficult to write with brevity, and that condensing a great many thoughts into a small space is a fine art.

It's therefore a great joy to watch Piet accomplish this here for 91 devotions, concluding with Psalm 91. Contrasted all the way through are the condition of the saints in our mortal bodies—incomplete, disguised, transient, in motion without having fully arrived—with the Lord; not only is He eternal, and complete in Himself, but He meets us in our temporal limitations and reveals Himself to us. Our pilgrimage on this earth, and the blessed diversions of our journey have a sure destination in our eternal home, and the present instant has meaning in the light of His eternity. I hope you enjoy reading and considering these meditations as much as I have.

Chris Godfrey

LETTERS *for* CHRISTIANS

EVERYDAY INCOMPLETE

PREFACE

Everyday Incomplete is the second in a smaller format pocketbook series titled *Letters for Christians,* and is a companion for the first in the series called *Everyday Love*. Both are intended for readers of all ages and levels of Christian maturity. This contains 91 letters with the 91st being Psalm 91. It's we who write to THE LORD because HE'S our FATHER and we're HIS children. *Everyday Incomplete* is for those of us who know deep down there are things that remain to be done; who are mindful of the unfinished, forgotten, or unsaid because they understand how every day *is* incomplete. We should be encouraged to write our own letters to THE LORD. It's exercise for the mind and will strengthen our faith that way. As with *Everyday Love*, each letter ends with a short prayer to set the mind for when it's time for us to pick our own Bible up and explore the full context of GOD's word.

Blessings
—*may the Lord be with you always.*

Amen

LETTERS *for* CHRISTIANS

EVERYDAY INCOMPLETE

INTRODUCTION

Every day we are incomplete, as are our lives here in this world because HIS work isn't finished in us and we're not done being GOD's witness. There are many ways in which we remain incomplete—in denial of our shortcomings; in the trials we've faced; temptation given into; and in not giving thanks for something asked for and received. It's easy to ask and even easier to forget we've asked. Being born again in the SPIRIT reconnects us with the LIVING GOD through JESUS CHRIST our LORD but our race isn't run and we're to remain connected to make sure we finish it in HIS grace. Psalm 91 is confirmation of THE LORD's protection against dark forces that want to break our connection. It reminds us that, while everyday incomplete, we remain protected every single day—with the promise of a day to come when we'll have finished the race. Until then every letter we write to THE LORD is incomplete. But the more we go back to each letter the closer we're drawn to GOD until that day when HE will be able to show us HIS salvation.

Lord, help us finish our letters to you.

Amen

EVERYDAY INCOMPLETE

1
FORTRESS

Psalm 91 points us towards our fortress JESUS CHRIST—our complete and eternal protector. But there is another fortress—a mental fortress—which we all struggle with. It's filled with everyday things that we expect to see because we see them so often. We expect to see a reed swayed by the wind; we'd be dismayed if a single reed was unmoved. In the same analogy JESUS asks if a prophet should be dressed in fine clothes to satisfy our respect for them. We should ask ourselves the same question today because in over 2,000 years we don't appear to have learnt a thing. There is nothing complete about us or in the things we do.

Lord, teach us to break from the mental fortress that so often snares us.

Amen

LETTERS *for* CHRISTIANS

2
NO SECRET

It's been said that the secret to happiness is not to focus on a person but on a larger project. The project presumably then makes everyone involved happy as individuals. It's an interesting idea that describes how infatuation with a single person can be overcome in this world by directing our energy away from them to something that includes them but in a broader sense. One could even extend the argument to our faith. If we substitute happiness for salvation, we could say that JESUS is our focus and the church, the larger project. Conversely, the church is one entity and thus our focus, while JESUS represents us all, i.e. the larger project. They're not mutually exclusive.

Lord, thank you that you're there for us both as a focus in our prayers and to share in.

Amen

EVERYDAY INCOMPLETE

3
BLANKS

A book arrived today which was opened excitedly only to see that, apart from the cover and the last page, all the other pages were blank. As the disappointment rose around the table there was one person who looked at it with anticipation. "Oh, it's blank, you see, so we can write our own story!" In a way we're all a bit like this book. We're the front cover and the final page of our life has been printed but we're excited about filling in all the blank pages in between. Everyday incomplete—we're a book and every page is a fresh start with our story ready to fill its pages.

Thank you Lord, that we're authors in our own life because you've given us the freedom to choose. Give us wisdom as we write, for when it's time to turn to the last page.

Amen

LETTERS *for* CHRISTIANS

4
RACE TRACK

A train dissipates air sideways as it's greeted by shuffling feet; above us the reverse thrust of aircraft engines howl vertically. There's a distant siren travelling westwards and cars protest a rule being broken further up the hill. These are all everyday sounds which don't even raise an eyebrow. It's simply organised chaos. Our race doesn't have anything to do with these sounds. Instead there's a warm smile to the left, condemned resignation ahead of us, alienation in the corner, and somewhere near the intersection stands loneliness. We have a race to run after being born again which has nothing to do with winning and everything to do with finishing.

Lord, we pray for wisdom to ignore what shouts at us and to see what doesn't.

Amen

EVERYDAY INCOMPLETE

5
THE RACE

Everyday incomplete—we rush at the strangers we meet,
*   for what it is they may unseat*
*   from the endless worries we entreat.*

The strangers are objects that can't speak,
*   yet brightly they shine*
*   and quick on their feet.*

They move our minds with great conceit,
*   in cunning confusion, sadness replete.*

Block our ears! Guard our eyes!
*   —it's the fallen one in keen disguise.*

For there is but One whom we should seek,
*   with all our heart, soul, and both feet.*

For Him we must complete the race
*   set for us in our meet*
*   when born again we were set free*
*   if ever there was a love so sweet.*

Lord, may we be wise to the useless idols crowding in on our lives.

Amen

LETTERS *for* CHRISTIANS

6
BLESSINGS

We're born alone, we die alone and there's nothing we can do about it; or, at least, not without GOD. In a way death completes us while in life we're incomplete, a work in progress. Yes, we're born again of the SPIRIT but we're a work in progress because our lives are now there to be used by GOD, however it pleases HIM. Being incomplete through the mercy of JESUS CHRIST OUR LORD is a rich blessing indeed.

Lord, may we always be thankful that we're a work in progress.

Amen

EVERYDAY INCOMPLETE

7
BACK ROADS

Highway maintenance is never ending. There's always a section of road that needs to be closed off for repairs and it's always just before Christmas or at the start of the school holidays. To get anywhere means we all pile on to the main highways, ignoring the back roads that are twice as long (and which take us to places we'd never think of going to). Our walk in faith can be a similar experience. When we're born again we rush on to the highway because we want to see all the important destinations as quickly as possible. But it's often the case that THE LORD doesn't want us there, preferring instead we take the back roads because of the places we wouldn't normally visit.

Lord, help us understand the importance of life's back roads.

Amen

LETTERS *for* CHRISTIANS

8
FRESH START

People like the idea of a fresh start—a re-birth of sorts— which is what New Year's Day represents, while New Year's Eve is the 'free hit' which pre-empts it. And yet when it comes to a new spiritual start the idea of being born again isn't as attractive. Why do it once when it can be done every year—and on our terms, an unbeliever might say. Many Christians are indifferent to the last day of the year and despite our brain trying to convince us otherwise, we're equally indifferent to New Year's Day. Indifference is a form of incompleteness and many of us feel neither complete or renewed by these celebrations, just fatigued because of its meaninglessness. There's nothing complete about time no matter how we categorise temporal events. So, while we should try not to be indifferent we should also avoid attaching meaning to the meaningless. There's simply the truth.

Lord, may we be focused on the truth, your truth.

Amen

9
WILL

We make our will for what's incomplete. Our lives are then, in one sense, completed by others. For some, this means continuing on in the minds of those who we've left, while for others it's simply being dismissed from life. Fortunately none of this matters because the will we write has nothing to do with what we think we've written. Our lives are our wills, not what we've asked a lawyer to do—but what we've asked our FATHER to forgive.

Lord, may we keep our eyes on writing a will that pleases you.

Amen

LETTERS *for* CHRISTIANS

10
DISGUISE

We are all guilty of having worn a disguise. Women have traditionally used makeup while men have focused on trophies to disguise themselves. Women are often a man's trophy and men are often trapped by a woman's beauty. But the truth is that women can be beautiful and men can be winners in GOD'S KINGDOM, without having to disguise themselves. Both are winners and both are beautiful in GOD'S eyes.

Help us to free ourselves Lord, from the trap of having to disguise ourselves in this world.

Amen

EVERYDAY INCOMPLETE

11
POTHOLES

There's a pothole with our name on it. It's the one that's always forgotten until we drive through it with a loud bang leaving half the suspension behind. In our spiritual lives we're faced with the same problem: our pathway blocked by 'incomplete roadworks.' Sometimes it's best if we just get out the car and fix it ourselves. THE LORD loves it when we help ourselves.

Lord, help us to help ourselves through faith in action.

Amen

LETTERS *for* CHRISTIANS

12
WORDS

Ambition. It's one of the most divisive things we may come across and yet, on the surface, is an innocuous word. Personified by Shakespeare to represents the negative aspects of everyday incompleteness, its hold on people can't easily be quenched because it's continuously demanding, selfish, and threatening. Ambition is personified in many ways, none more so than in the glossy corporate boardroom scenes where success is measured by the size of one's smile. It has the potential to produce creatures of light and charm who've embraced evil. But we're also reminded in the Bible of two instances where ambition is valuable: in preaching the gospel and for leading a quiet life.

Lord, lead us safely past the temptation to be ambitious in this world but rather to be ambitious to serve you.

Amen

EVERYDAY INCOMPLETE

13
CITY

Cities personify incompleteness. They're never exhausted. Even as midnight rolls on over towards the new dawn there's no end to the activity it generates; nor in its morphing physical presence. The saying that when we're tired of London we're tired of life, is true in a sense of all cities because cities never tire and when we've become the city we are its life—and its death. Believers are fortunate not to fall for the ideas spawned about the might of cities. The only city we look forward to serving in is GOD'S new HOLY CITY prepared as a bride for us, HIS church.

Lead us Lord, towards your new city.

Amen

LETTERS *for* CHRISTIANS

14
ORDINARY

Taking the dog for a walk is something that has to be done and it's permanently incomplete. No sooner is it back in the house than it's angling for another walk. Dog walks can sometimes be the most boring repetitive task in the world. Except when they're not. We often expect exciting things to happen as Christians and when we're faced with repetition we're often left slightly out of sorts. But THE LORD wants us to look at everyday things—incomplete, ignored, and uninteresting though they might be.

Help us Lord, to understand the importance of everyday life.

Amen

EVERYDAY INCOMPLETE

15
MANUAL—MATIC

Manual or automatic. That's the choice we have when buying a car. Some of us like to have a choice about everything in our lives while others prefer a lifestyle where decisions are made for them. Neither of these two options are ideal. Both produce difficult people. The first type are overbearing and demanding of life while the second type underachieve and are frustrating to deal with. THE LORD can deal with any personality type but HE also cherishes those leaders that are somewhere in the middle: people that can be decisive while also able to stop and listen.

May we be decisive and bold Lord, in listening as well as doing.

Amen

LETTERS *for* CHRISTIANS

16
ONE LIFE

Daylight savings forces behavioural change in people—and that's just from tweaking the rules a little. But despite moving hours around we're still struggling with how incomplete each day is. It seems no matter how we rearrange the furniture there's simply not enough hours in a day. That's the mistake we make. We're consumed with fitting life into 24 hour shifts when life is a single shift progressing incrementally: past to present. The future is not life because it's not here yet.

Lord, help us to tackle our lives differently—as one single working day.

Amen

EVERYDAY INCOMPLETE

17
LEAVING

We're always leaving. That may sound like an odd thing to say but taken in an everyday incomplete way it's true because we're never with anyone all of the time. Always in and out the door, in another room, or just not in any meaningful conversation. We come and go as do the people around us. So, it's true to say we're always caught somewhere leaving someone. It's life: everyday incomplete. But THE LORD never leaves us even when we think HE has.

Lord, how magnificent your love for us is.

Amen

LETTERS *for* CHRISTIANS

18
ARTEFACTS

Walking around a museum can be inspiration for one reason which is not always obvious at first. It's basically a room full of incomplete artefacts. Isolated they stand, naked to the gaze, their story impossible to tell properly. They're incomplete because they've been taken out of their original context which no longer exists and yet here they stand as part of everyday life. It's an inspirational place to hang out in because it's when standing in the middle of it all that we realise how utterly insignificant we are. But it's the next thought that speaks to the glory of GOD, because we're everything to HIM, if only we turn away from worshipping HIS creation to worshipping the creator himself.

Lord, may we never forget who we worship, a most fearful and wonderful God.

Amen

EVERYDAY INCOMPLETE

19
EMPTY CHAIR

A cynic might say that life is a game of musical chairs but we can be forgiven for looking at the empty chair in a room for what it signifies: what's incomplete—in a family, in a relationship, or even in a person. There's always an empty chair for someone arriving or because someone's left. To see an empty chair hurts for a reason: so that we might pay attention when the chair is taken.

Lord, we rejoice when it hurts because it means we're thinking.

Amen

LETTERS *for* CHRISTIANS

20
NOW!

How many times have we stood impatiently in front of a clock watching the second hand ticking away, or in front of a microwave oven watching it count down second by second. The wait is excruciating. How long it takes! Why then do our lives run out so fast? The answer is found in the things we pay attention to. GOD wants us to be aware of what time it is because how else is HE able to catch our attention and to say " Watch out now!", "Get ready now!" or "Now!—do this!".

Lord, help us to watch as the seconds slowly pass so we're able to stop the years fly by.

Amen

EVERYDAY INCOMPLETE

21
TO BE COMPLETE

The unique thing about our lives is that we're always moving even when we think we're not. The earth's rotation has us in constant motion. It's as if to stay alive we need to be in motion and the moment we stop we're no longer alive. We are therefore always changing, always incomplete. And in another kind of motion, every second of our lives is already in the past. We can't ever claim to be in the present for no sooner is the claim made than it's already claimed by the past. Now compare our existence with GOD who is unchanging because GOD is eternal and eternity is to be complete.

Lord we're constantly moving, always incomplete—until your will is done here on earth as it is in heaven.

Amen

LETTERS *for* CHRISTIANS

22
IN OUR MIDST

Clouds are visually transforming elements in a constantly changing atmosphere. The atmosphere represents what's out there and we're protected by its downward pressure. The higher we go the less protected we are. So why, one could ask, do we want to go higher and higher. It's because we're led to believe that GOD is out there somewhere and so if we could somehow go to 'out there...somewhere' we might find HIM. But THE KINGDOM OF GOD is here in our midst.

Thank you for reminding us Lord, where to look for you.

Amen

EVERYDAY INCOMPLETE

23
SUNNY DAYS

No-one cares where the light switch is on a bright sunny day but as evening approaches it's warm glow can be seen and during the night we're grateful to have it on so that we can see what we're doing. GOD's light is always on but when everything's going well we often don't notice it at all. Why would we when we don't need it. Our lives are bright enough, we think. It's when darkness approaches that we start sitting up and taking notice. Then, in the pitch black of night, we run towards the light, hoping and praying that it'll stay on. THE LORD knows how we are—HE's been one of us—but HE looks to bless those who see HIS light, even on a nice sunny day.

May we always seek you Lord, especially when things are going well.

Amen

LETTERS *for* CHRISTIANS

24
REALITY

Every day is incomplete, then forgotten when the next day arrives—which also ends up incomplete. It's the same for all the days that roll by. It's the reality of how we live life and it's difficult not to feel saddened by this pattern of inevitability as yesterday's news becomes tomorrow's. It explains all the shiny objects that keep us distracted from knowing how incomplete we are. GOD can only recognise us if we recognise ourselves and to do that we must repent of all our sins, be born again, and accept the HOLY SPIRIT. That's the reality: GOD'S reality.

Thank you Lord, as you help us face up to your reality.

Amen

EVERYDAY INCOMPLETE

25
UNDERSTANDING

Knowledge is a wonderful thing—until it no longer applies because we've learnt something new which disproves what was known before. Our thirst for knowledge comes at a price if we lose sight of understanding. When we understand what knowledge *doesn't* mean, then we're in a better place to observe wisely. Knowledge is what we think we know about the cause of an illness but understanding is able to cure it. Knowledge is the encyclopedia while understanding is knowing which two pages to look at together in context. Knowledge means we're able to recite the Bible verse for verse but understanding is the ability to look at someone's heart. Knowledge is incomplete—we can tire ourselves out with learning; but understanding revitalises us, the fruits of which are faith, hope and love.

Lord, give us the wisdom that understanding provides, we pray with thanksgiving.

Amen

LETTERS *for* CHRISTIANS

26
BE THERE

There was a time when it was virtually impossible to communicate without having to physically go to a person, wherever they were, and look them in the eye. Today technology has connected us in all sorts of ways—but hasn't it only made us feel more incomplete than ever?

Lord, help us keep contact with one another in a meaningful way.

Amen

EVERYDAY INCOMPLETE

27
THE BOAT

How often have our prayers been incomplete because we've not found what we've been looking for. Doesn't THE LORD understand?—we think to ourselves. Like being out all night and not catching any fish. The solution was not to go further out or to some other location, but simply to throw the net out on the right side of the boat. Sometimes we just need to do something differently when we've hit a brick wall because what we're looking for is right there next to us.

Open our eyes Lord, to the possibilities around us when all seems lost.

Amen

LETTERS *for* CHRISTIANS

28
MEANING

In politics people come and go, as they do in the commercial, social, and religious world. There are important people, so important that we think they're worthy of great distinction and even irreplaceable. Surely GOD will have noticed fine people such as these, we think. The reality is different from the reality we think we're witnessing because all these people have no meaning except for their heartfelt repentance. The only meaning we ever have in this world is when THE LORD intervenes for us—and what meaning that has!

Praise the Lord because our importance lies in the safety of his loving arms!

Amen

EVERYDAY INCOMPLETE

29
WOBBLY TABLE

Who hasn't been to a restaurant and sat down at a wobbly table. The solution varies but one way is to fold a paper napkin or business card and stick it in under one of the legs so that the table is at least steady, if not horizontal. Most of us do this without thinking because we like fixing things, but some of us would prefer to avoid the problem by asking for another table or going somewhere else. Going to church is a bit like that, where something in the tone or content of the message becomes irritating. We could either get up and leave or grin and bear it. Or, we could make a few mental adjustments and enjoy the rest of the service. People who are able to mentally adjust, even if they disagree with something, are far more valuable to GOD than people who don't at least try. Of course, if the whole table is ready to collapse—if the message is a false teaching—then it might be time to leave, for good.

Lord, help us to be patient in life—but not patiently foolish.

Amen

LETTERS *for* CHRISTIANS

30
NEW HORIZON

Any vista can look completely different after a snowstorm but as the snow melts, the view returns to what we're used to. In certain conditions we can be transformed like that—in the joy of a wedding or sorrowful funeral. But we always return to our normal self soon after—the transformation incomplete. It's humanly impossible to be transformed unless we've been covered in GOD'S snow. The snow is like HIS grace and we're changed forever—as has the view we have on life.

Lord, only you can complete us by changing what it is we see.

Amen

EVERYDAY INCOMPLETE

31
TINY

We scurry around on this earth, tiny little creatures chasing dreams; our desires caught up in lust, violence, and search for idols. We hide our true self from everyone, thinking in a microscopic vacuum about... ourselves. We aren't even here long enough to achieve anything—and then we're gone.
Tiny.
Little.
Creatures.
What is it about us that GOD so loves? The answer may lie in what our minds are capable of as we, having been made in his image, can move mountains from here to there with the faith of a mustard seed. One day we'll understand but for now all we need to know is that GOD cares for us because we're made in his image and it's not because we can build cities. The city GOD cherishes is the one we build in our minds, with HIM, in THE KINGDOM OF GOD. Hallelujah!

Lord, we understand nothing except that your grace is enough for us now.

Amen

LETTERS *for* CHRISTIANS

32
OUR JOB

One of the best things to happen to us can be that we lose our job. The problem with some jobs is that it makes us feel as if we're complete. It's a trap because we stop thinking and invest all our energy in one place: the wrong place. GOD wants us to think about HIM all the time and HE wants us to invest in all HIS ways—in faith, hope and love. That doesn't mean we lose out on life. It means we become rich beyond measure.

Lord, help us chase our dream, which is to know you better.

Amen

EVERYDAY INCOMPLETE

33
VICTORY

Bravery and loyalty are strange companions. If you've ever been on the ground watching a group of skydivers, it all seems rather pedestrian, or at least doable. All that's really needed is a bit of courage. But when we're up there in the plane looking down it's a different story. Suddenly we need massive amounts of courage. Loyalty is an even more fickle emotion. It's easy to say but as we're asked to be loyal or expect loyalty from someone else in increasingly difficult circumstances, things change quickly. To give our life for someone is both an act of bravery and loyalty. It's the ultimate sacrifice and accolade we're able to earn and it's almost always done in war, but never for our enemy. JESUS' death on the cross exemplifies both bravery and loyalty. HE willingly died for those who hated HIM, for who HE loved and, in the spiritual battle, to forever defeat HIS enemy.

Lord, we look no further than you for the definition of bravery and loyalty. Praise your Holy name!

Amen

LETTERS *for* CHRISTIANS

34
LET'S GO HOME

Let's go home. How often haven't we said or heard it said. Home is the place where we feel most secure. It has little to do with where, how big, or how comfortable and beautiful it is. Sometimes home can be a dangerous place but we'd still like to go because it's *our place*. For a Christian home has a special significance because we've never been there, we don't know where it is, and we're not sure who our neighbours are. But that's because we're comparing it to what we know to be our home here on earth. In CHRIST we never have to say "Let's go home" because we're already at home, secure in HIS love.

Lord, thank you that we're able to call you home.

Amen

EVERYDAY INCOMPLETE

35
WHAT NOT TO DO

'To do' lists are a good way of getting things done but sometimes we rely on them too much and our brain starts becoming lazy—in the sense that we can't seem to remember to do anything on time without the list. Technology has that affect on us too. Will we one day forget how to pray properly or become infatuated with biblical horoscopes? The convenience of modern technology is a double-edged sword because there's a ransom to pay. Having given it the power to push us around we've now reached the point where, if we want to opt out, we'll be excluded from society. We should get comfortable with the idea of being excluded from society if we're to resist this bully because beyond that point lies the road to hell.

Hear us when we call for help Lord, and show us what to do.

Amen

LETTERS *for* CHRISTIANS

36
AMBULANCE

An ambulance is easily recognisable. We know immediately from the shape, colour and sound what it is and what it represents. When an ambulance stops at a neighbour's house we naturally start assuming the worst and if we can, we'll watch to see if we can get an idea of how bad things are. We also start thinking about ourselves because we know that one day it might stop at our house. But we shouldn't be surprised because we've had an ambulance arrive for us before, when we were laden with sin and unable to process any of it—as our lives just got heavier, darker, and more desperate. That ambulance was JESUS.

Thank you Lord, for arriving just when we needed it most—we can now never forget your intervention in our lives.

Amen

EVERYDAY INCOMPLETE

37
SELF-MADE

There's much to admire about self-made people and their reputation can be a little overwhelming. Abraham and Lot can be considered archetypes of self-made people but the distinction is that Abraham made it his mission to trust GOD while Lot trusted in himself. In truth neither were self-made, being entirely reliant on GOD's mercy at all times. But Abraham considered himself incomplete while Lot will have considered himself complete, evidenced by his own actions. Haven't we at times brimmed with pride after some or other accomplishment and, even if it wasn't said out loud, felt that we'd 'arrived,' that we were complete. What a dangerous place to be in!

Lord, guard what we say, do, and how we feel when driven by pride.

Amen

LETTERS *for* CHRISTIANS

38
ONE LIGHT

Christmas lights have a certain jolly brightness about them and then there are warning lights, on top of buildings and construction cranes, which are stronger, more intense and can be seen for miles. Even stronger are aircraft, ambulance, and police lights which are impossible to ignore. All these lights are warnings but are not harmful. But there is a light so powerful that Moses had to warn his people to stay away, so holy that we dare not look, and so intense that the radiant face of Moses had to be covered until the effect of his meeting with GOD had worn off. This light will one day be all we need in our new city.

Praise your name Lord, for being the light in our lives.

Amen

39
PROFESSIONALS

The difference between a professional and an amateur in any field is easy for all to see. There are also professional Christians who differ from most of us due to their dedication and intellect. They are the lighthouses that warn us against disaster. They're not prophets because a prophet's mind must be cleared of intellectual debris but they're mighty in GOD's army and guardians of HIS word. We should treasure these people for all the work they do behind the scenes.

Thank you Lord, for unsung heroes who work tirelessly behind the scenes to protect your Word.

Amen

LETTERS *for* CHRISTIANS

40
PRIDE

Pride is a terrible sin. It's difficult to pinpoint and harder to acknowledge. We can be so arrogant that we don't recognise it in ourselves. It wreaks havoc on relationships, silencing some and raging in others. Putting two proud people in a room is to be surrounded by despair. Add ambition, mix in vanity and what's left is a recipe for disaster. THE LORD detests all the proud of heart.

Lord, may we quickly strike pride from our lives lest it consume and condemn us before we know it.

Amen

EVERYDAY INCOMPLETE

41
THOUGHTS

The most frustrating thing sometimes are incomplete thoughts. We never know we've had an incomplete thought until some time later when, for some reason, we're able to return to it and maybe even try to finish it in the direction it was originally going. Our dreams are full of incomplete thoughts but while awake we're expected to think things through properly. For Believers, changes in thought often mean THE LORD is guiding us away from or towards something. But not always. Sometimes we're meant to have followed through with a thought. How do we know? By listening to our teacher: THE HOLY SPIRIT.

Lord, our thoughts can run away from us; help us bring them back through the power of the Holy Spirit.

Amen

LETTERS *for* CHRISTIANS

42
ENERGY

We live in a collection of boxes we call a home, with electricity running around each 'box' to each and every electrical outlet—in the walls, floors, and ceilings. But we don't really think of it in those terms—as living in a powered up cage. We just see a plug point which means energy supply. The current will kill us if we make contact without being isolated properly and yet we're nonplussed by this surrounding force. For us, THE HOLY SPIRIT is our fortress. We're isolated from harm because we've accepted CHRIST as our SAVIOUR. The force surrounding us is the mercy we've received—it's always there for us if we stay true to HIM.

Thank you Lord, that we know the source of our power.

Amen

EVERYDAY INCOMPLETE

43
PERSEVERENCE

Fishing requires perseverance and it's no accident that it's one of the most memorable themes in the New Testament. The analogy can be taken for everything we do in life because it's a personification of our earthly struggle. It's hard not to notice the waning interest of those around as we struggle to make sense of what THE LORD has asked us to do. Many nights we'll drift off to sleep knowing how little progress we've made; and in the morning we wonder whether we should try something else. But the one thing about being incomplete at the end of every day is the knowledge that we have to persevere—keep fishing—because joy is just around the corner and it's there for us to catch.

Thank you Lord, for teaching us to persevere especially on those dark nights when its hard to see all the fishing boats around us.

Amen

LETTERS *for* CHRISTIANS

44
WORTHY

Internet groups, full of anonymous people gathered in the digital town square, are interesting places to exchange ideas because they're full of all types of people. It's a murky digital world as words on a screen are all we have to go by. But it's also a positive thing in that we're not intimidated by a person's reputation or social standing because we don't know who they are. They might be a friend or an enemy. In one sense then we're all on a level playing field and it's the ideas being discussed that count. THE BIBLE is like that: a level playing field. Anyone can read it and the heart wins every time.

Thank you Lord, that your word is a level playing field because we're all worthy if we repent and are born again.

Amen

EVERYDAY INCOMPLETE

45
WANT

Greed, when our eyes are bigger than our stomach, is often applied to food but it's really relevant in anything that speaks to our attitude to life. 'Wanting it all' is another way of putting it. The problem with wanting it all is in the 'all.' The more we want in life the more there seems to be of it and how many of us have found ourselves at the end of our lives, deflated and tired of wanting things. Before we were born again, wanting was why we got out of bed in the morning but it's different for us now because 'want' has been replaced by *want to*. We want to please GOD; we want to be like CHRIST; and we want to live in faith, hope and love.

Lord, we want to be useful to you here in this world.

Amen

LETTERS *for* CHRISTIANS

46
OLD HABITS

Who hasn't come across a born again Christian who's been imperfect in their behaviour? Some habits and behaviours are hard to change. Being born again doesn't mean old habits disappear, it means repentance, forgiveness, and then to go and sin no more. But what about those nasty habits? The difference is that where we once enjoyed sinful behaviour we now don't. We're new creatures living by his mercy but we're still incomplete—a work in progress. If anyone claims to have been born again and never sinned since, they're not to be trusted. To *not* want to sin is our daily prayer and one day we'll be complete but until then we have JESUS.

Lord, the one prayer you probably hear most often is a sinner's prayer and we ask that you walk us through those prayers each and every day.

Amen

EVERYDAY INCOMPLETE

47
PERSONA

In looking back on this past week, was there a time when we felt complete? It would be surprising if any of us felt complete. Most of us will have experienced multiple feelings of incompleteness. Nor are these feelings of inadequacy limited to ordinary people. Comedians are known to be very different in real life. The same too for politicians as well as many other professions that require a different personality in public life to be successful. But a follower of CHRIST isn't like that and if we come across anyone who is, it would probably be best to stay clear of them.

Lord, forgive us when we pretend to be something else in front of others.

Amen

LETTERS *for* CHRISTIANS

48
SURPRISE

So many Christians who think themselves complete have much to say these days. "We've been saved!"—they shout. "We've been blessed!"—they cry. "There are no more surprises!"—they claim. It's true that we're not to be surprised by many things: the need to be born again; a world that doesn't care for us; the trial we're to endure—and yet many of us will be surprised when JESUS returns. Did we feed HIM, clothe HIM, visit HIM in prison, in sickness help HIM? Did we look for those who are incomplete, just as we ourselves are, or did we just celebrate our own salvation?

Lord, remind us every day of what you expect from us—so we too may never be surprised.

Amen

EVERYDAY INCOMPLETE

49
MEASURE

With a ruler we can measure and give an object extra information we didn't know before. To see a table is one thing but to know its dimensions means we understand it better. The table hasn't changed but by defining its size we've given it a place in this world which is more durable than before. Now it's a table we understand better. We 'measure' everything in life because it's our job to give as much meaning to the things we interact with. We 'measure' people too but in a different way—tacitly—such as 'long brown hair,' 'blue eyes,' and 'a smile that lasts about 3 seconds.' GOD measures us in this way too but HE'S able to measure qualities which we can't comprehend in other people. That's why, when it comes to spiritual well-being, only GOD is able to understand and it's best we not judge a person according to how 'good' or 'bad' we think they are. They may be a heartbeat away from salvation or from destruction and only GOD knows this information.

Lord, forgive us when we judge others.

Amen

LETTERS *for* CHRISTIANS

50
PLUGS & KEYS

For things to work in our lives we need all sorts of plugs for all sorts of objects from toasters to mobile phones. We also need keys for things like cars, doors, and safes. What would we do without plugs and keys? Both unlock something for us, namely, use. A plug is like a key in that it securely unlocks the electricity we need; while a key is like a plug because it securely unlocks the affordance that an object provides. They're both ordinary everyday objects but are almost indispensable in our daily lives. Everyday objects in Believers lives are GOD'S word and prayer. Prayer unlocks the power we need while GOD'S word unlocks the use of that power.

Thank you Lord, for your power and for teaching us how to use it.

Amen

EVERYDAY INCOMPLETE

51
PRECIPICE

It's taken some time getting used to robots. Comic books and science fiction films got us all going, but it's taken a bit longer to get beyond the fantasy. Now with the advent of electronic hand-held devices, those people with their faces buried in their mobile phones are de facto in a robotic state. And the state is growing. Who needs artificial intelligence when our minds have been distracted by cute phone apps as we stand on the precipice of a new revolution, the hybrid human: part man, part machine. None of this should be news to anyone though. But where do we all stand in relation to GOD's word? It's hard to tell how much more obscene life is to become before GOD's patience runs out. We should, by now, all be paying attention and helping one another unravel the levels of deception confronting us. John watched and wrote it down and we've been told to keep watch too.

Lord, help us to keep watch as we find ourselves in a fast moving environment full of disturbing new developments.

Amen

LETTERS *for* CHRISTIANS
52
ROCKS & BANKS

Great rivers, having reached their destination, end quietly—a long way beyond what were once fast flowing waters crashing against rocks and banks. Many of us die in this way too, our groan an incomplete disguise of our once bold, carefree selves. If there was ever a time when we felt complete it would have been at the height of our youth when we too were crashing against life's rocks and banks. And if anything shaped us as people it would have been those same rocks and banks, testing our resolve when we were young and strong.

Lord, thank you for our youth because that's when you could see the best and the worst of us.

Amen

EVERYDAY INCOMPLETE

53
A VIEW

Views are just that—parts of something more complete. All we have throughout our lives are views, each an incomplete picture of a much larger picture and yet how desperately we argue sometimes that our view represents the whole picture!

Forgive us Lord, when we insist that only we are right.

Amen

LETTERS *for* CHRISTIANS

54
FEEDERS

Bird feeders are great to watch. The birds don't need them but they're a luxury hard to ignore. We don't need them either but watching these birds makes us feel good. There are lots of things in life we don't need in a particular moment but they also make us feel good. Praise, presents, respect, achievements—they're all little luxuries which we could manage without but they enrich our lives and THE LORD loves it when we're living rich, rewarding lives. Which is why HE has HIS own feeder for us. We're able to fly up to one at any time and fly off feeling enriched and cared for. It's HIS WORD through THE HOLY SPIRIT. And there's no need to buy any seed.

Lord, may your holy name be praised for giving us the spiritual boost we need.

Amen

EVERYDAY INCOMPLETE

55
FRACTURES

A crack in the wall could mean several things. It could just be from drying out too quickly; the difference between two materials; or tiny horizontal breaks from infrastructural settlement. The worst cracks are the result of clay where the soil heaves between being dry and soaked. Those deep angular fractures are angry, ugly marks because of the stress involved and the only permanent solution is to rebuild the entire wall and supporting foundation. It's the same in people where stress causes an inflamed reaction which is hard to douse. It keeps responding to differing conditions just like the clay soil. It's the kind of fracture which is incomplete and often it's best to rebuild their lives in JESUS. That's why when we're dealing with difficult people it's often useful to know what type of fracture they have.

Lord, give us the wisdom to know what kind of intervention is required in people's lives.

Amen

LETTERS *for* CHRISTIANS

56
FALSE HEIGHTS

Given a choice most of us would want to live on the top floor of a building especially for the views. It's also nice to know there's no-one above us. The vertical relationship describes life on earth because we attach an importance to how 'high' we are in relation to others. But in GOD's kingdom what matters more is the horizontal relationship, with THE LORD's most important people on HIS right hand side and from there we're all spread out around HIM in countless numbers according to the book of Revelation. The distinction between horizontal and vertical is an important lesson for us all because to be like JESUS requires we look outward to our neighbours, not down at them.

Lord, help us to remember where our neighbours are to be found.

Amen

57
MIRACLE

There are many people, including Christians, who don't like Christmas at all. Apart from the fact that it's not THE LORD'S date of birth or that it's been overrun by pagan ritual and symbolism, Christmas is also a time of grief, loneliness, depression, and anxiety. Where many families thrive at Christmas time, many others have imploded. Whether we like this time of year or not, we should perhaps focus on the day we were born ... *again*. Because that day is a marker of HIS miracle, where as sinful as we were, HE saved us. For CHRIST was born so that we could be born again!

Lord, we bow down to you in gratefulness for the special day we were saved.

Amen

LETTERS *for* CHRISTIANS

58
MADE RIGHT

We've all seen those movies where someone is transported back in time and has to adapt to a previous time period. What would we do if we were transported back to JESUS' time. Would the first thing we look for be a USB charger or bottle of water? How different would we really be after getting over the lack of an air conditioned supermarket within spitting distance? The incompleteness in life isn't that the objects around us have changed but that we haven't—because we're all still essentially the same people as at any time in history. But just as GOD's people were made right with GOD then, we're made right today through HIS new covenant.

Lord, thank you for your everlasting mercy regardless of the time period we lived in for you alone know our hearts.

Amen

EVERYDAY INCOMPLETE

59
PALIMPSEST

Like a palimpsest our lives can be summarised by the numerous attempts to start over again, or fix mistakes made, and then writing a new story on top of the old story board. But traces of the old still remain no matter how hard we scrape away at the past. At the end of our lives, as one experience has replaced another, we're left with a record which has many layers to it. But if we've accepted CHRIST as SAVIOUR we're handed a new board on which to write; and every time we falter, another new board is handed to us. Forgiveness is a wonderful thing and it gives us the confidence we need in writing our story so that it ends up becoming part of HIS story.

Thank you Lord, that our old sins are forgotten and forgiven.

Amen

LETTERS *for* CHRISTIANS

60
MESSAGES

Sending a message to the wrong person is something we've all done. Then there are those tacit messages we send which are not so obvious except of course to a person who's on the same wavelength. The British, for example, have a keen sense of humour and have a way of saying things, or rather not saying things, to each other that many foreigners don't grasp. The parables in the Bible are an example of JESUS saying things which HE knew people wouldn't understand because their hearts had hardened against HIM. But the message of salvation was unambiguous and those who had ears and a full heart, heard it.

Lord, may our messages to those around us about you be clear and unambiguous.

Amen

EVERYDAY INCOMPLETE

61
LOUDSPEAKERS

The problem with many hearing aids is that all they do is amplify the sound instead of defining the sound better. "It's like having a pair of loudspeakers in your ear" someone once said. We're often guilty of simply increasing the volume when talking to someone who's being stubborn about GOD's forgiveness. What's needed is to leave the script at home and take the time to choose the right words and speak them with care.

Lord, may we take care in how we talk to others about you.

Amen

LETTERS *for* CHRISTIANS

62
PATIENCE

Cricket is a game a lot of people don't like and one of the reasons is because it's not understood. A batsman stands out there and waits. They wait and watch patiently as ball after ball goes flying by or gets blocked with their bat or pads. Then suddenly it's smashed through the field on the way to the boundary. A bowler also bowls ball after ball, watching, waiting. Fielders watch and wait as the bowlers and batsmen watch and wait. Sportsmen and women make some of the best Christians because they're patient, brave, and able to soak up huge amounts of stress without complaining. GOD loves people like that. They're everywhere in the BIBLE and they can teach us a lot about watching and waiting.

Lord, thank you for those around us who teach us about watching and waiting.

Amen

EVERYDAY INCOMPLETE

63
OUR LIGHT

It's not possible to get a pure white colour by mixing paint; it's only possible when we mix red, green, and blue light waves. So, what the earth produces can't produce white but light can. Light is a theme that runs throughout the BIBLE especially in the New Testament and is most often used to describe the effect GOD has on us. GOD is indescribable but HE is our light and HE shines brightly in a very dark world.

Thank you Lord, for being the light for us in this world.

Amen

LETTERS *for* CHRISTIANS

64
FRIENDS

Friends are valuable precisely because they're not permanent. There are friends we want to fight for, friends to laugh with, to drink with, for comfort, and to play sport with. There are even 'friends who aren't really friends.' But the most important friends are the ones we want to worship with and those are precious and hard to find.

Lord, send us more friends who we want to worship with.

Amen

EVERYDAY INCOMPLETE

65
DISAPPEAR

When we see a person walking in the distance and they disappear behind a tree, just because we can't see them doesn't mean they're not there. And when they re-emerge we aren't in the least surprised, having mentally tracked them until they reappeared. Death is a bit like watching someone disappear from sight for a short while. But they're not gone, just out of sight.

Lord, we can't see you but we know you're always there.

Amen

LETTERS *for* CHRISTIANS

66
TRAINING

We're all trained to do something in life. A carpenter works with wood; a chef with food; fishermen catch fish; a welder works with steel. When it comes to solving problems we tend to use what we're trained in to get to a solution. But if there's not enough wood, food won't solve the problem, going out in a boat won't find wood, nor would welding two steel plates together. Life throws curve balls and we have to adapt to new circumstances. However, there is training that can solve any problem but we have to start as apprentices. It's to be fishers of men and there's always work to do.

Lord, teach us your ways so that we too can be fishers of men.

Amen

EVERYDAY INCOMPLETE

67
+1

It's quite sobering to think about JESUS in certain situations and on some of life's stages. Walk into any pub—would we see JESUS there? A rock concert—where would HE have sat? Christmas lunch—who would HE have sat next to? Monday morning team meetings, Wednesday's fitness class, Friday drinks. Every week, year after year. We may think there's no way JESUS would have been in any of these situations but can we be sure? Wherever we go HE'LL be with us because we've asked HIM into our lives. The question really is not what we're doing in some of these places but whether we're introducing HIM to those around us. Or do we squirm a bit inside when HE'S next to us? Our response to these kind of questions is the most important thing in our lives. Is HE our +1 or are we HIS?

Lord, may our response to life's questions grow in maturity until we no longer disappoint you.

Amen

LETTERS *for* CHRISTIANS

68
CANDLE

The light of a candle must be one of the most tender things to watch as it flickers on and off, barely visible at times—but always fighting for its life. We can lose ourselves in its tiny light as well as find great joy in its feeble warmth. Perhaps we see ourselves in a candle. Most of us take great care keeping it alive. We like watching its wax drop away forming those soul–soothing shapes. There's a reason that candles are still present in our churches as well as Christian artwork. They do something to us and for us. They make us think deeply especially in quiet surroundings. There's nothing quite like being in an isolated beach house lit by one or two candles at night. We see our own frailty reflected back at us making it much easier to go down on our knees in prayer. In its incompleteness a burning candle represents everything that modern life has forced us to turn our backs on.

Lord, we pray that you will watch over us no matter how frail our light may be.

Amen

EVERYDAY INCOMPLETE

69
WATER

Water can change its appearance from liquid to steam and condensation; or to ice and snow. But its still composed of the same elements. Other things can only change state in one direction, for example, when we stir sugar into a cup of coffee we can never separate those elements again. It's hard not to think of how some transformations can be reversed while others are irreversible. Our relationship with GOD is composed of the same kind of transformation. We're either sinners but it's reversible or we're sinners and our state of mind can't be reversed. We can be saved or we can refuse to be saved and at some point our decision will 'stick.' We can't have it both ways. We go in to bat for THE LORD or we're in the opposing team.

Keep us safe Lord, from being irreversibly condemned, we pray.

Amen

LETTERS *for* CHRISTIANS

70
MIXED RESULTS

Salt and pepper shakers are normally identical, differing only by the number of holes at the top. The tradition has been for salt to have a single hole and pepper three small holes but there have been times when someone's covered their food in pepper thinking it was salt. As Christians we often think we're helping a situation by adding just the right 'seasoning' but we've grabbed the wrong shaker and it's just making things worse. All it needed was for us to pay attention when grabbing what we thought was the right strategy when dealing with people.

Lord, help us to be more sensitive to other people's needs.

Amen

71
JEALOUSY

Jealousy has to be one of the most difficult sins to overcome. Along with its bedfellow, envy, and distant cousin, rage, it has the potential to destroy lives and doesn't take much to catch fire. Jealousy of partners, siblings, relations, friends, co-workers, and neighbours is an emotional cancer: difficult to detect early and often accompanied by benign symptoms such as mild irritation. The problem with psychological threats such as jealousy is that they can't be diagnosed in the same way a medical condition can. We must rely on THE HOLY SPIRIT to warn and advise us about how to overcome this insidious condition.

Lord, protect us from psychological threats such as jealousy.

Amen

LETTERS *for* CHRISTIANS

72
FALSE LIGHT

The devil moves with lightning speed, his camouflage complete as he seeks to devour people by destroying relationships. We should all take great care to say what we mean and mean what we say because the evil one is like odious liquid, seeping in wherever it can and rotting everything from the inside where no-one can see. Our only hope rests with CHRIST's eternal love and it is HE who, if we call on HIM, breaks us free from every alienating force. Light is the one form of camouflage used with devastating effect in this world by the devil because he mimics everything GOD does. We're to resist the devil by putting on the full armour of GOD.

Lord, our hope rests in your eternal truth and we pray that we'll stay the course, following only your way.

Amen

EVERYDAY INCOMPLETE

73
APOLOGY

Sometimes we're not good friends to others; sometimes friends are not good to us. But if we're grounded in the truth it doesn't really matter for too long because we'll have a chance to apologise, as will they. But apologies only ring true if they're meant and we should take care around people whose behaviour isn't reflected in an apology; just as we need to be sincere in our apologies to others. There's no point in apologising but continuing with behaviour that caused the problem in the first place. The only way to get right with people is to get right with THE LORD because HE is truth. The rest will follow.

Thank you Lord, for having set the perfect example of how we should be.

Amen

LETTERS *for* CHRISTIANS

74
THE NARROW

Some of the nicest paths are long straight sections while others are winding. It seems that when it comes to pathways it's not so much what kind of path it is but how wide it is. In the narrower pathways we see more of life in the edges, textures, and adjacent relief. It would be difficult to imagine someone enjoying a stroll down say, an airport runway. The path we take to be reconciled with GOD is a narrow one and although it might not be as easy to walk on, we're enriched by the scale of our everyday experiences. It's narrow enough to pay attention to every detail along the way.

Thank you Lord, that we're able to walk on the narrow path.

Amen

EVERYDAY INCOMPLETE

75
SAVED SOULS

Dividing time up into days, months and years is done to establish order in society. We all now have a reference point for everything we do. But GOD doesn't need this reference point. Creation is explained by the six days and a day of rest but HIS days aren't our days. We should be careful not to put too much emphasis on our definition of time or on the way we've agreed amongst ourselves to order society because we may trap ourselves by limiting our understanding of GOD's power. Celebrating a calender is meaningless to GOD. What has meaning is that we've turned back to HIM. We should all remember that GOD counts saved souls—not days, weeks or years.

Lord, help us to remember how your time is not our time.

Amen

LETTERS *for* CHRISTIANS

76
DERELICT

There's nothing more depressing than walking past a once thriving business that has closed down and now lies empty or derelict. At night these buildings are especially sad and lonely places. If we've ever worked in or been part of the life of one, it's a distressing sight. The distress however wouldn't be for the architecture, machinery, or location as much as for the missing people because we were the life in them. This earth without people would be the same as an abandoned building because GOD has no use for it except for who HE's put on it.

Thank you Lord, that we are so special to you.

Amen

EVERYDAY INCOMPLETE

77
THE 'A' TEAM

Nature has much to teach us, not least of which is to work together. Outside on any day we might see the 'odd couple': a parakeet and a pigeon. The pigeon arrives first, shuffles up next to a small hand mirror placed in between two plants and waits patiently, every now and again flirting with its own reflection. Then, on time, the parakeet arrives, bright green and with lots to say. The pigeon says nothing as the parakeet starts swinging on the feeder directly above, every now and then craning its neck down towards the pigeon. Then the pigeon starts feeding on the seed that's been falling down next to it. After a short while both fly off until the same time the next day. All that's left of the scene is the feeder swinging itself to a standstill. We may sometimes need someone else to do something before we can do what we need to do.

Lord, we pray for the ability to work together and support one another in your name.

Amen

LETTERS *for* CHRISTIANS

78
BEING USED

Most everyday objects perform better the more they're used. The more traffic over a tarred surface, the better. Dental fillings perform better the more they're chewed on. Car engines need to be driven. A house needs to be lived in. It's the same for people. The more interaction we enjoy, the friendlier we generally become. And in faith, the more we exercise spiritually the more we're able to endure, the further we can run, and the greater our chances of finishing the race.

Lord, help us to use all you've given us to better effect.

Amen

EVERYDAY INCOMPLETE

79
ADDICTIVE

We tend to think of addiction in terms of drugs and alcohol because they're quite easy to spot, but things like behaviour can be addictive too. We can become addicted to being around someone who makes us laugh because it tempers levels of stress in us. The point is that it's when our minds are enslaved that we're most at risk because the outward signs are hidden, often even from ourselves. Then combine these types of addiction and we've become a bit of a mystery novel that's hard to unravel, for example, alcohol and laughter are possibly one of the most addictive combinations out there. It's good to know that GOD's word doesn't enslave, it sets free.

Thank you Lord, for setting us free.

Amen

LETTERS *for* CHRISTIANS

80
HOLIDAYS

If there's one thing that's incomplete, it's a holiday. A holiday is over almost before it begins and yet it's almost never over because the memories are always in play. Holidays seem to take forever to start but before we know it we're slamming doors to go home. And in between is just a blur. Just like life. It takes forever to become independent, then a blur, and then we're dependent again. The curious thing is we don't see the shortness of life as a warning that we should find our salvation in THE LORD.

Lord, if life is like a holiday, help us make the most of it because it is so brief.

Amen

81
WHAT IF

If we were able to go back in time to do things differently, the single thing most people would change is to not fear others. Maybe, if we'd kept on at something instead of backing down because someone reacted negatively to our efforts, we'd have succeeded in doing what we enjoyed. But then again maybe if we'd stood up to peer pressure and got to know THE LORD earlier or known HIM better we'd have avoided a lot of heartache. It's an impossible regret to bear and all we can really do is to be grateful that we got to know THE LORD when we did, were able to sincerely repent, and could call on HIM for protection. Because whatever road we might have chosen, we'd still have needed HIS protection from this world.

Lord, thank you that despite all our weaknesses we've been able to get to know you.

Amen

LETTERS *for* CHRISTIANS

82
STARTING AGAIN

We're never too old to start again. Our lives can be changed in the wink of an eye, and often are. Political winks, business nods, religious prompts—all can have a devastating effect on ordinary people. There aren't many Christians who haven't suffered from plans made by vain, cruel leaders, and have had to start again. Some with one suitcase between them standing on a platform in the middle of nowhere, going to somewhere they've never been. Others stripped of ownership, of the means to produce, and caught up in No-Man's Land for years. But starting again for a Christian means everything.

Lord, starting again with you means everything to us.

Amen

EVERYDAY INCOMPLETE

83
WHO WE ARE

The characters blessed by GOD throughout our BIBLE appear to be very different to one another. Some seem to be very difficult people; others, very calm. Some challenged GOD while others were humble and reserved. Some sinned greatly and even murdered while others appear to have always been full of respect. Some were hotheaded and foolish; others cool and wise. But regardless of their personalities they were all incomplete. Christians nowadays seem to be afraid of being themselves. It must be a sin to not be ourselves and yet many of us strive to be like someone else.

Lord, thank you for accepting us as we are and keep us from trying to be someone else.

Amen

LETTERS *for* CHRISTIANS

84
THE END

Having unfinished business is different from being incomplete. Unfinished business implies that there's an injustice that needs to be addressed. We Christians are incomplete but we don't have unfinished business because THE LORD took care of injustice on the cross. It's in the heavenly realm where the unfinished business remains. The forces of darkness must still be held accountable and completely destroyed. Because when the great accuser is gone there'll be no-one left to taunt us for being still incomplete.

Thank you Lord, that we no longer have unfinished business.

Amen

EVERYDAY INCOMPLETE

85
OUR REFUGE

It can be argued that one of the most common themes in the BIBLE is that GOD is with us and we're not to be afraid. Psalm 91 is a good example of this. Just before this, in Psalm 90, we're encouraged to consider our own mortality. Psalm 91 reassures us of HIS protection because as feeble and fleeting as we are, when we trust HIM and seek HIM out HE will be our refuge and fortress.

Thank you Lord, that we can call on you in times of trouble.

Amen

LETTERS *for* CHRISTIANS

86
SPIRITUAL WARFARE

What type of danger could we be in? There's physical danger which we're always aware of and then there's spiritual danger, the type we don't think about as much. A big part of spiritual danger lies in accusation. Whenever we hear an accusation, it's not coming from THE LORD, but from forces of darkness. THE LORD wants to build us up, not break us down, which is why HE allowed HIMSELF to be sacrificed to atone for our sins. To have come from the cross and then to accuse us doesn't make sense. Every breath HE took was for forgiveness. We should never be misled into thinking that the accusations we face come from GOD. GOD doesn't accuse us, HE disciplines us. The devil accuses us so that we might be deceived and lose faith.

Lord, help us to know the difference between accusation and discipline.

Amen

EVERYDAY INCOMPLETE

87
ACCUSED

When we're accused and we listen to the accusation, how might we be deceived? If we're accused of being a bad Christian or a fake one, the first thing to suffer would be our self esteem and confidence. Then we might look around for a role model and be shown a wolf in sheep's clothing, good on the outside but evil within. We might be tempted to believe other false teachers and, being misled, could end up walking away from GOD. We might be drawn into a false church where THE BIBLE is misinterpreted on purpose. We might be lured by financial reward in return for supporting immoral behaviour. We might have sinned but are unable to get past the torment of the accusation. We'll definitely be told that we won't be forgiven. All these things will be thrown at us but we should know that THE LORD won't torment us—HE'LL fix us.

Lord, thank you that you're able to fix us when we're down and help us to learn to trust you to do that.

Amen

LETTERS *for* CHRISTIANS

88
FEAR NOT

Fear is real, or at least we think we know it's real. It can cripple us mentally and physically but it can also supercharge us. We can use fear to defend ourselves. It's transformation from a state of shock. Whether it's real for us or not we know that GOD hates it when we fear. HE loves fearless followers of CHRIST and it's easier to be fearless than we think. Just convert that state of shock into a state of faith. And that's what we have THE HOLY SPIRIT for, to prepare us in advance, to help us stand and remain standing. Our refuge, our fortress, our source of strength is the same today as it was in Moses' day—and it's what we must use to conquer fear. When we cry out to the Lord we needn't be fearful because whatever happens, HE'S got us safe in his arms.

Lord, fear is a strange experience but it's just an experience. Help us overcome what's not real with what is: You.

Amen

EVERYDAY INCOMPLETE

89
GOD'S CHURCH

A spirit level is used to check how perfectly horizontal or vertical a surface is but if what we're trying to measure is too large, it won't give us an accurate reading. In the same way, our minds are able to measure some of the reality of this world but we can't comprehend dimensions infinitely more complex so we're incomplete until we're able to see these. We can't measure surfaces in a church because GOD'S ways confound man's. The measure of a church is evident by the levels of forgiveness it contains, not the straightness of its edges and only THE HOLY SPIRIT can measure these. The metric used is forgiveness because to be like CHRIST is to forgive; it's an act of love. So, in the spirit of forgiveness, it's only when the last member of the last congregation finds their place that the church will be completed by JESUS CHRIST our LORD AND SAVIOUR. We're to run our race until then, with joy.

Praise God for His grace and mercy!

Amen

EVERYDAY INCOMPLETE

90

DEAR LORD

Psalm 91 is a comforting song of prayer which helps us get to know you better Lord. Help us to write better letters by reading them back; then thinking about *why* we wrote what we wrote; and finally having a look at what your word says in the Bible. What we've written may make perfect sense but then again it might make us think a little bit more about where we stand with you Lord. Help us to reject accusations as soon as they appear and to joyfully watch as those dark clouds evaporate in an instant. All it takes is to stand and remain standing. When we hear you say, "Let's fix this" then we know you're right beside us.

What a blessing you are to us Lord. What a comfort! The day will come when we'll be complete. Until then you are our fortress in these confusing times.

Amen

LETTERS *for* CHRISTIANS

91
PSALM 91

1. Whoever dwells in the shelter of the Most High
   will rest in the shadow of the Almighty.
2. I will say of the Lord, "He is my refuge and my fortress,
   my God, in whom I trust."

3. Surely he will save you
   from the fowler's snare
   and from the deadly pestilence.
4. He will cover you with his feathers,
   and under his wings you will find refuge;
   his faithfulness will be your shield and rampart.
5. You will not fear the terror of night,
   nor the arrow that flies by day
6. nor the pestilence that stalks in the darkness,
   nor the plague that destroys at midday.
7. A thousand may fall at your side,
   ten thousand at your right hand,
   but it will not come near you.
8. You will only observe with your eyes
   and see the punishment of the wicked.

EVERYDAY INCOMPLETE

9 If you say, "The Lord is my refuge,"
   and you make the Most High your dwelling,
10 no harm will overtake you,
   no disaster will come near your tent.
11 For he will command his angels concerning you
   to guard you in all your ways;
12 they will lift you up in their hands,
   so that you will not strike your foot against
   a stone.
13 You will tread on the lion and the cobra;
   you will trample the great lion and the serpent.

14 "Because he loves me," says the Lord, "I will
   rescue him;
   I will protect him, for he acknowledges my name.
15 He will call on me, and I will answer him;
   I will be with him in trouble,
   I will deliver him and honor him.
16 With long life I will satisfy him
   and show him my salvation." (NIV)

Amen